A LINE A DAY
SIGHT READING
By Jane Smisor Bastien

D0128188

Preface

A Line a Day Sight Reading, Level 1 may be used after a student has been exposed to all of the notes on the staff. Concepts from *Bastien Piano Basics, Piano, Primer Level* (WP200) are reinforced in this book.

Each page has two parts:
- a line of notes ("Daily Note Search") to name and play in the correct place all over the keyboard. These notes are out of position.
- three four-measure phrases to sight read. Only C, G, and Middle C five-finger positions are used.

It is recommended that the student complete the "Daily Note Search" *each* day and then play *one* four-measure phrase correctly with as little "practice" as possible. Specific directions are given on page 2. Transposition of the four-measure phrases may be assigned if desired.

The following Primer Level books are suggested for further sight reading.
Favorite Classic Melodies (WP72)
Folk Tune Favorites (WP46)
Nursery Songs at the Piano (WP241)
Popular Hymns (WP226)
Popular Christmas Songs (WP220)
First Pops for Piano (WP135)
First Songs of My Country (WP140)
Piano Recital Solos (WP64)
Happy Halloween (WP103)
Happy Valentine's (WP104)
First Parade of Solos (WP237)

About the Composer

Jane Smisor Bastien teaches pre-schoolers through advanced high school students in her La Jolla, California, home studio. She is very active in the San Diego music teacher organizations.

For many years Mrs. Bastien was director of the Preparatory Department at Tulane University in New Orleans. It was for her students there that she first started writing. Since then she and her husband, James, have produced music and methods for all ages.

ISBN 0-8497-9422-6

Daily Note Search

Name and play the notes in the correct place on the keyboard, holding each note for its exact value.
Use the most convenient fingering.

Before You Sight Read Each Phrase

1. What is the time signature?
   Write the counts in the book.
2. Look through the entire piece and try to discover any possible problem spots.
3. Notice the dynamics, slurs, and ties.
4. Find the hand position.
   What is the first note in the right hand?
   What finger goes on that note?
   What is the first note in the left hand?
   What finger goes on that note?
5. Set the tempo by counting one measure aloud and then play on the next "one." Play slowly enough so
   you can think about everything and keep a steady tempo.
   Counting aloud with the metronome ($\quarternote$ = 50) will help you keep a steady beat.

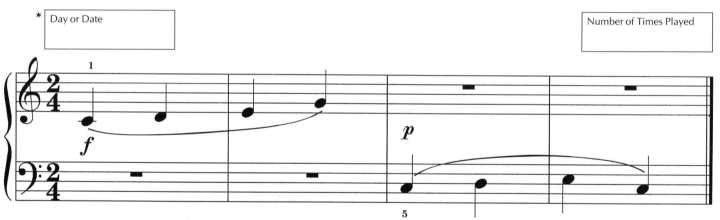

Evaluate Your Sight Reading

1. Did you play the correct notes?
2. Did you play straight through in the correct rhythm and keep a steady tempo?
3. Did you count aloud as you played?
4. Did you lift your hands to "breathe" at the ends of the slurs?
5. Did you observe the dynamics?

*Keep a Record of Your Progress

1. In the first box write the day, or date, you read this phrase.
2. In the second box check ($\sqrt{}$) how many times it took you to play it correctly.
3. Your goal is to have as few checks as possible.

For example:

Daily Note Search

1.

Day or Date	Number of Times Played

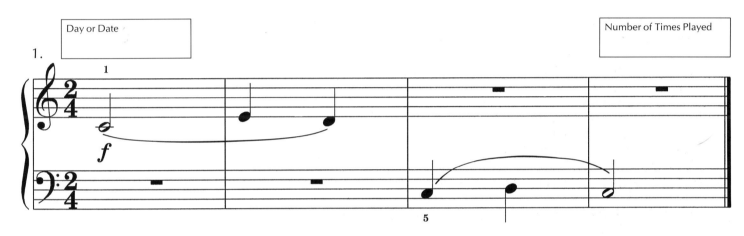

2.

Day or Date	Number of Times Played

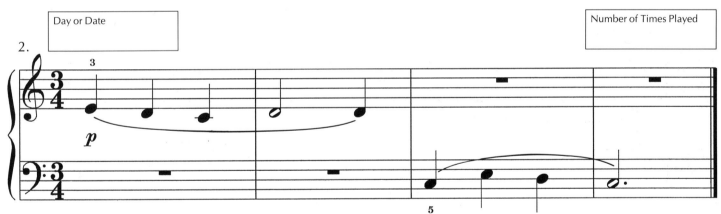

3.

Day or Date	Number of Times Played

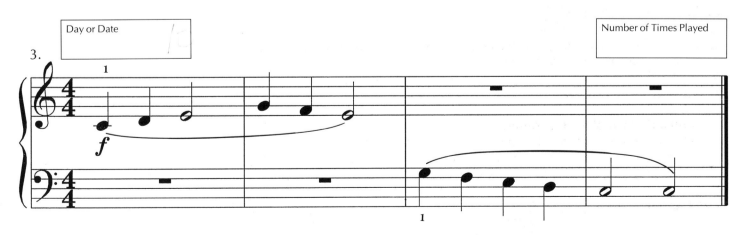

Daily Note Search

Day or Date

Number of Times Played

4.

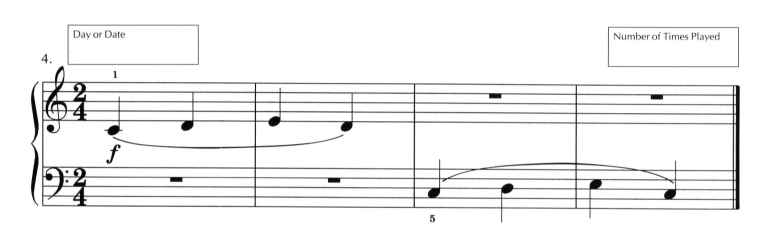

Day or Date

Number of Times Played

5.

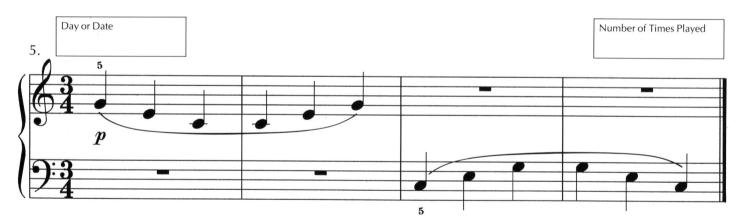

Day or Date

Number of Times Played

6.

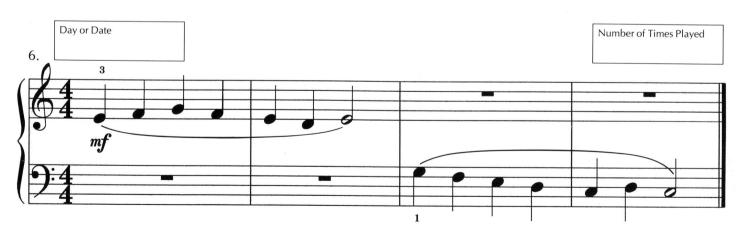

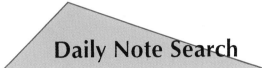

Daily Note Search

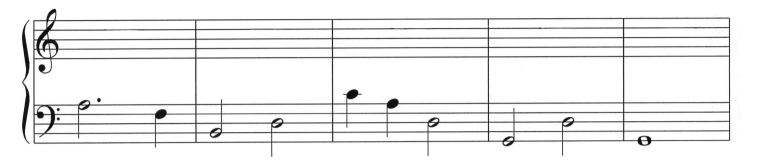

After you have sight read each line a day as usual, play lines 7, 8, and 9 without stopping. Now you are playing a long solo! What will you call it?

Day or Date		Number of Times Played

7.

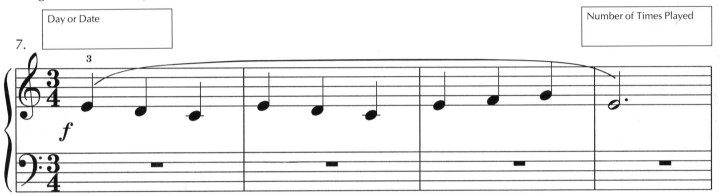

Day or Date		Number of Times Played

8.

Day or Date		Number of Times Played

9.

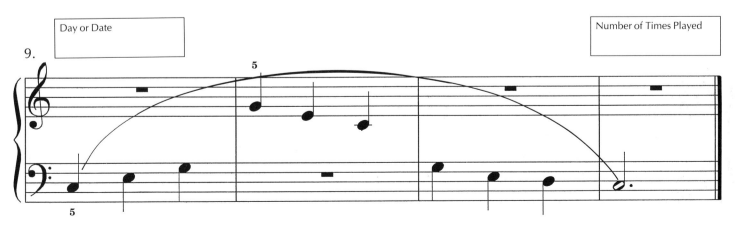

Daily Note Search

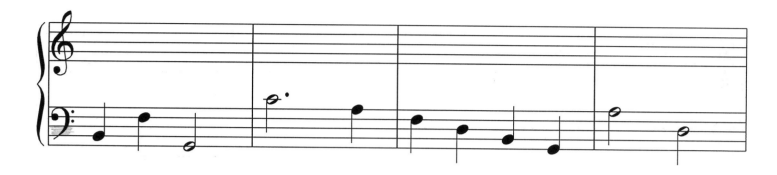

Day or Date		Number of Times Played

10.

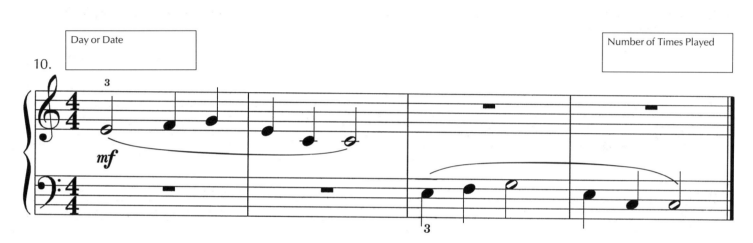

Day or Date		Number of Times Played

11.

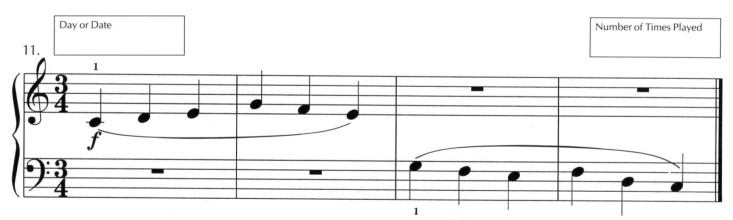

Day or Date		Number of Times Played

12.

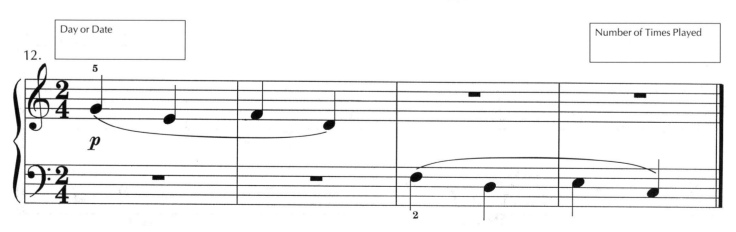

Daily Note Search

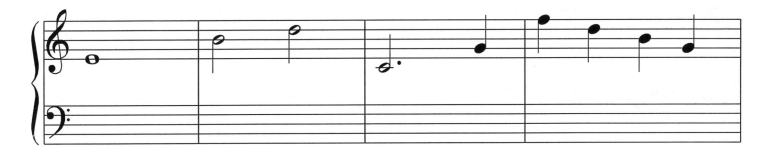

After you have sight read each line a day as usual, play lines 13, 14, and 15 without stopping. Now you are playing a long solo! What will you call it?

Daily Note Search

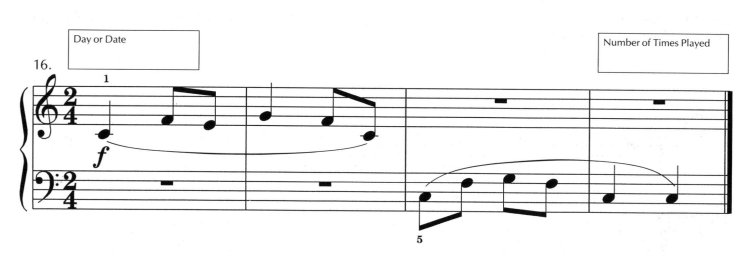

Day or Date

Number of Times Played

16.

Day or Date

Number of Times Played

17.

Day or Date

Number of Times Played

18.

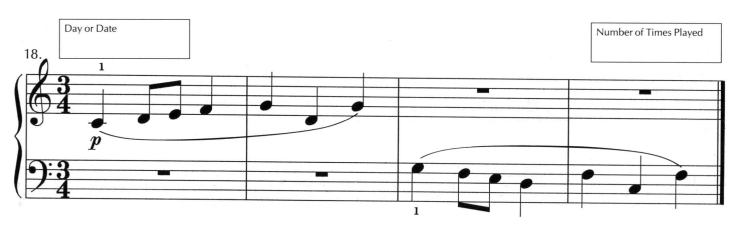

Daily Note Search

After you have sight read each line a day as usual, play lines 19, 20, and 21 without stopping. Now you are playing a long solo! What will you call it?

Day or Date		Number of Times Played

19.

Day or Date		Number of Times Played

20.

Day or Date		Number of Times Played

21.

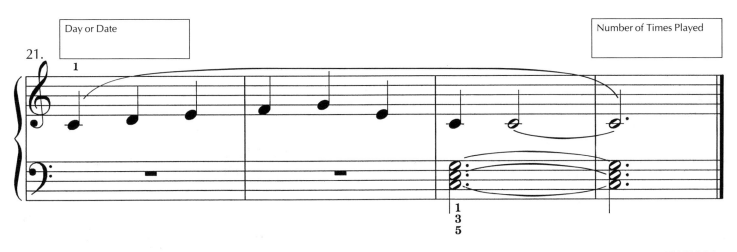

Daily Note Search

Day or Date

Number of Times Played

22.

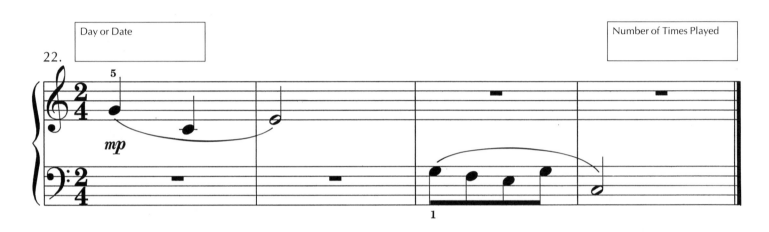

Day or Date

Number of Times Played

23.

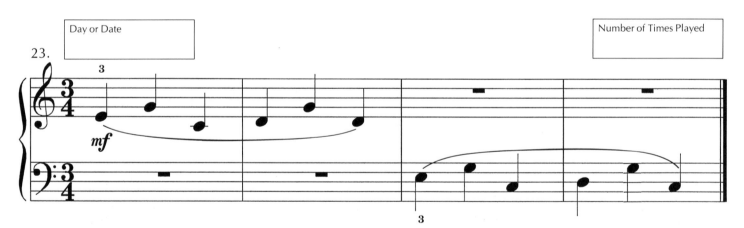

Day or Date

Number of Times Played

24.

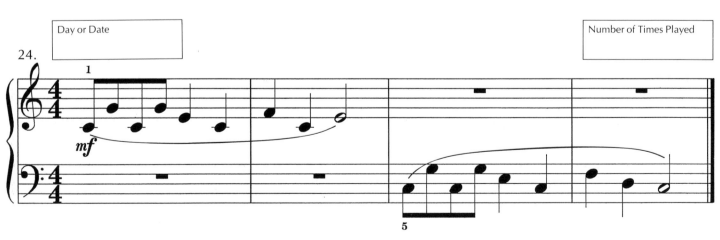

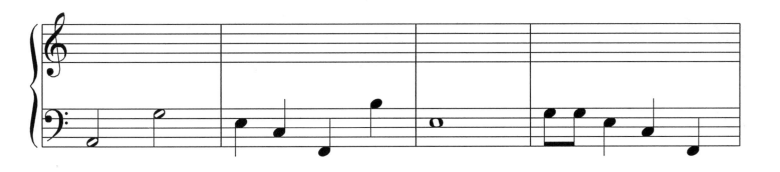

Daily Note Search

After you have sight read each line a day as usual, play lines 25, 26, and 27 without stopping. Now you are playing a long solo! What will you call it?

Test your sight reading on this longer piece!

28.

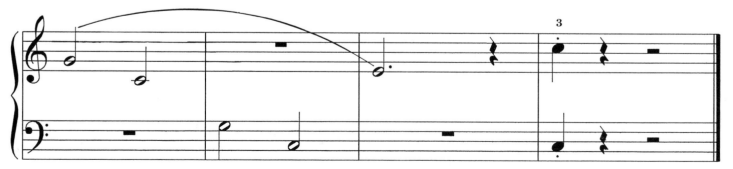

Daily Note Search

Day or Date

Number of Times Played

29.

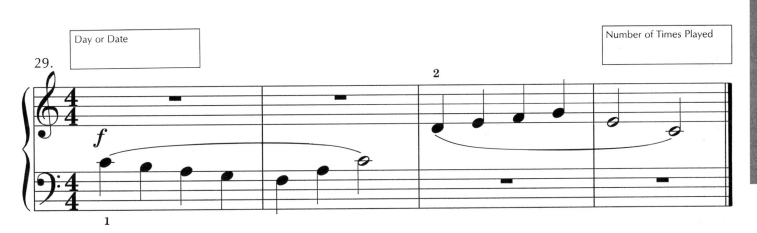

Day or Date

Number of Times Played

30.

Day or Date

Number of Times Played

31.

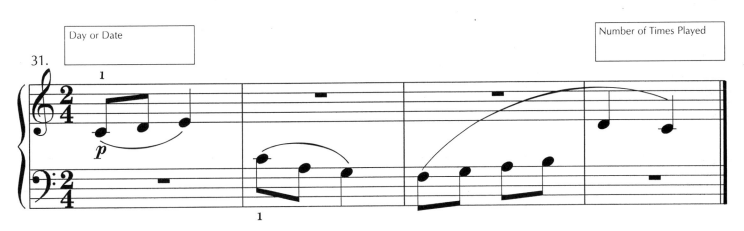

Daily Note Search

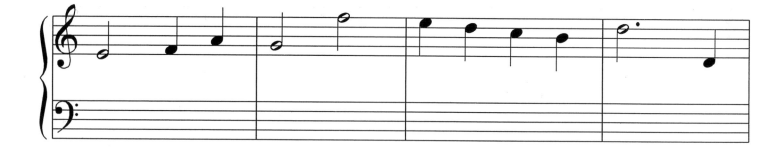

Day or Date

Number of Times Played

32.

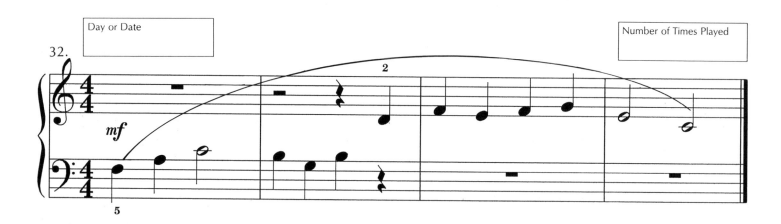

Day or Date

Number of Times Played

33.

Day or Date

Number of Times Played

34.

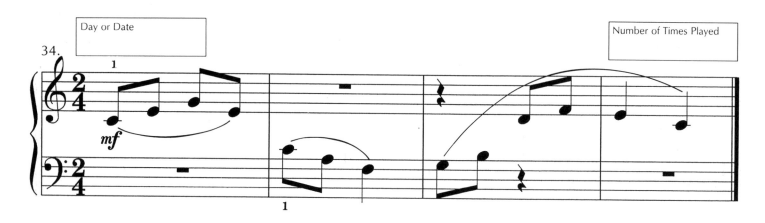

Daily Note Search

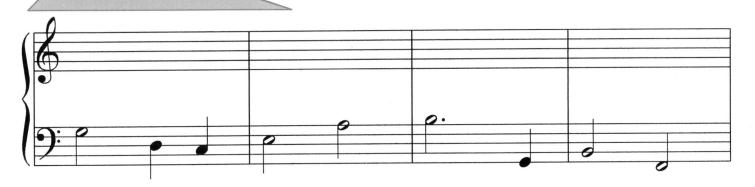

After you have sight read each line a day as usual, play lines 35, 36, and 37 without stopping. Now you are playing a long solo. What will you call it?

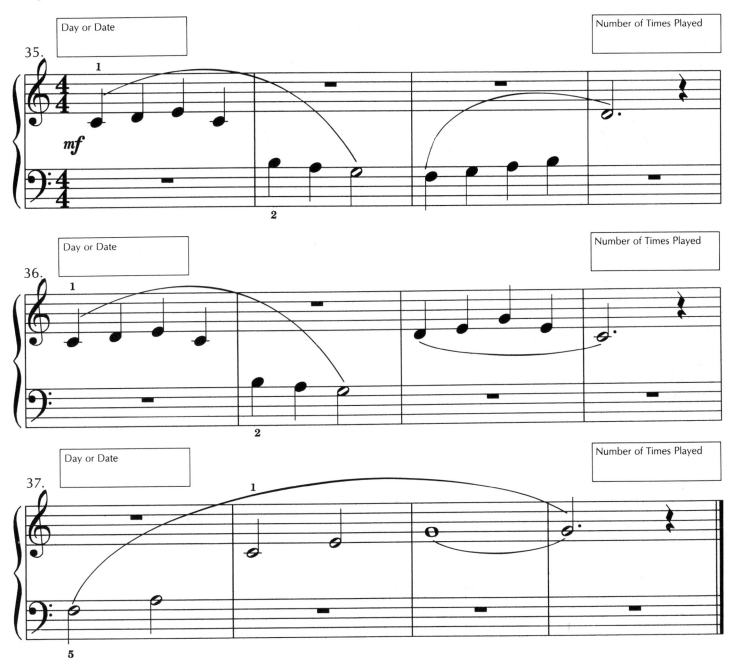

Daily Note Search

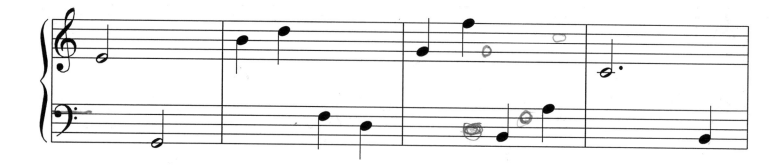

38.

Day or Date	Number of Times Played

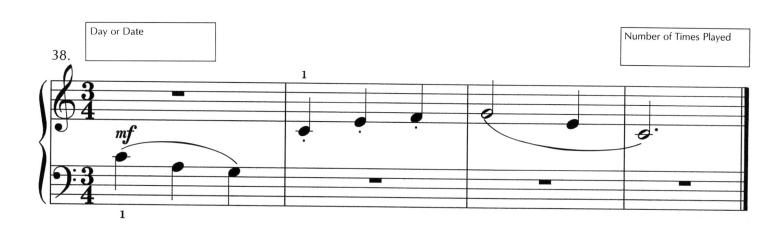

39.

Day or Date	Number of Times Played

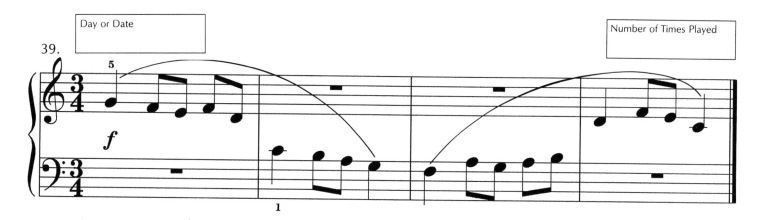

40.

Day or Date	Number of Times Played

Daily Note Search

After you have sight read each line a day as usual, play lines 41, 42, and 43 without stopping. Now you are playing a long solo. What will you call it?

Daily Note Search

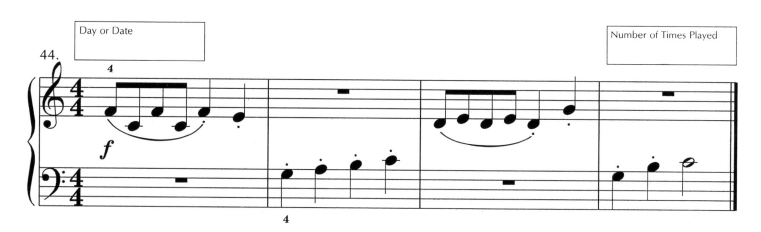

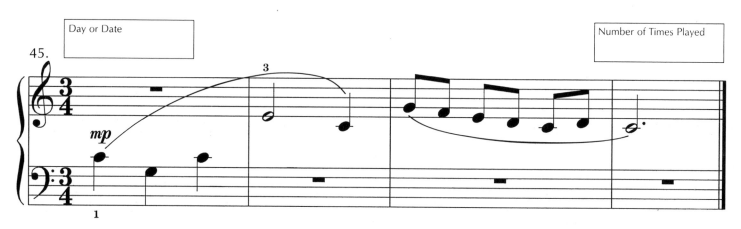

Daily Note Search

After you have sight read each line a day as usual, play lines 47, 48 and 49 without stopping. Now you are playing a long solo! What will you call it?

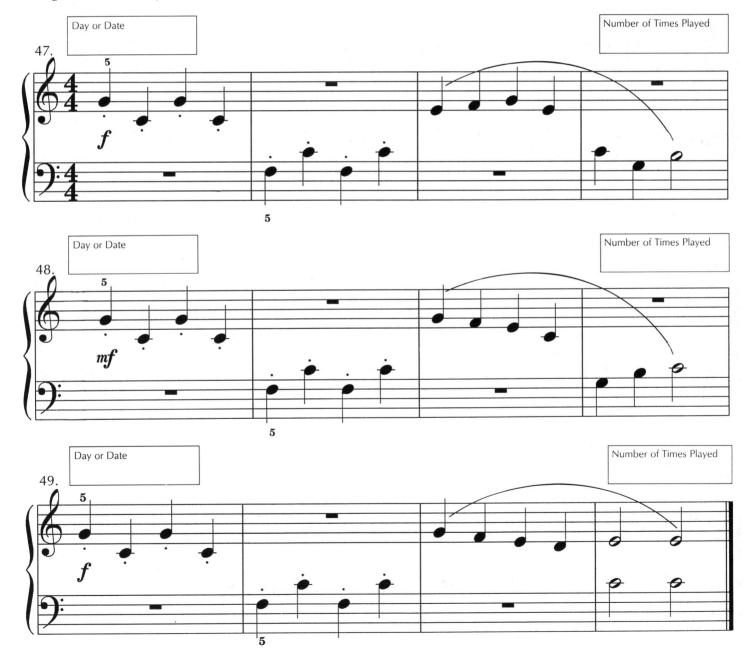

Daily Note Search

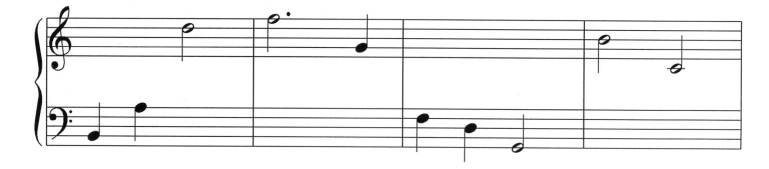

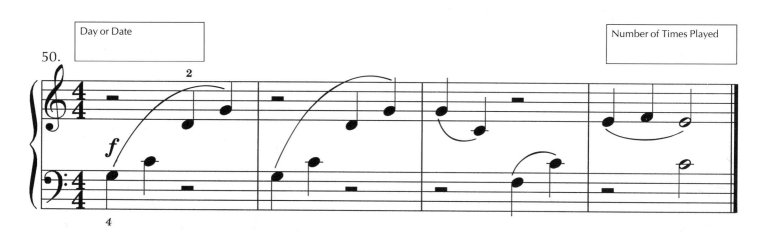

Day or Date

Number of Times Played

50.

Day or Date

Number of Times Played

51.

Day or Date

Number of Times Played

52.

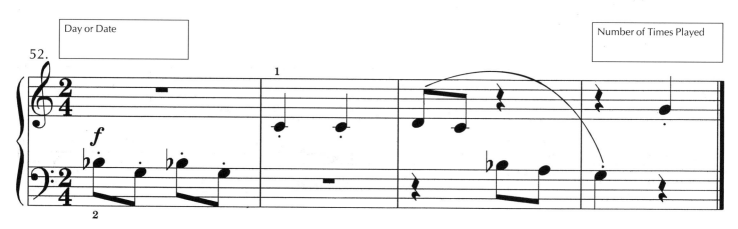

Daily Note Search

After you have sight read each line a day as usual, play lines 53, 54, and 55 without stopping. Now you are playing a long solo! What will you call it?

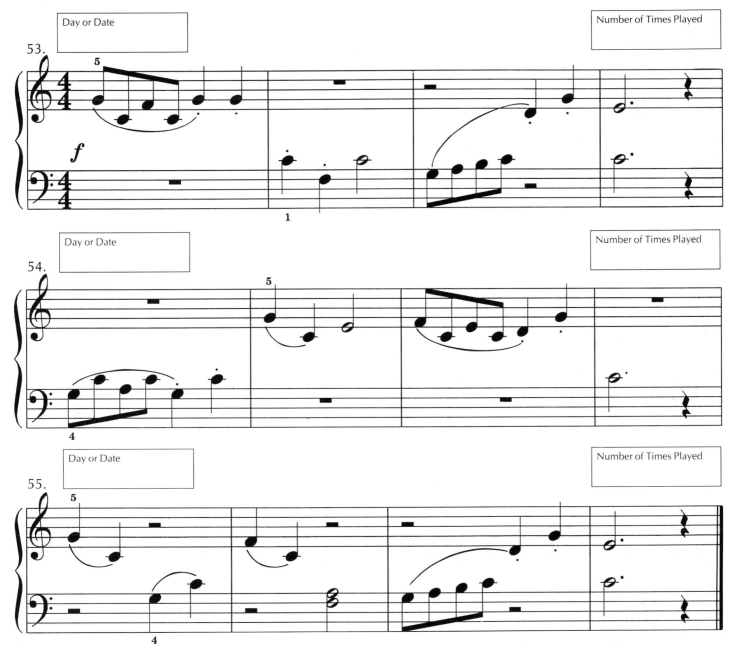

Daily Note Search

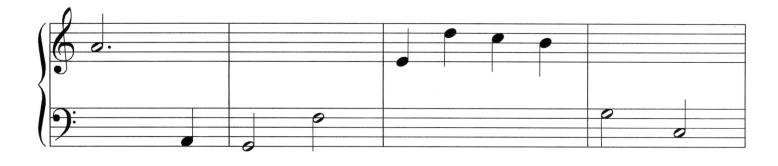

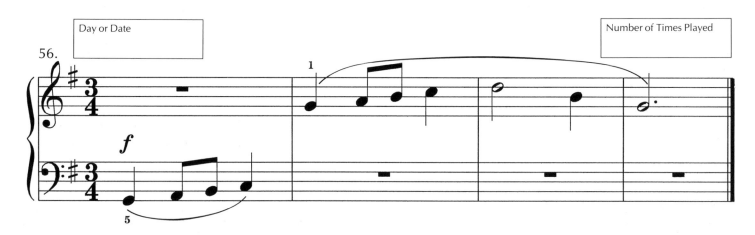

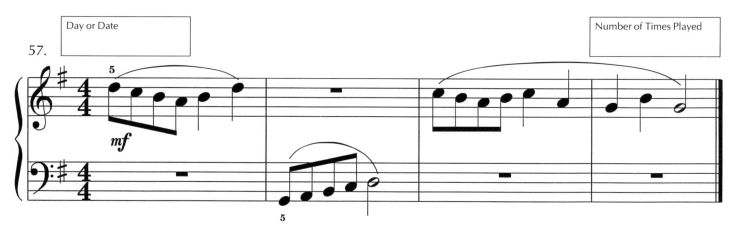

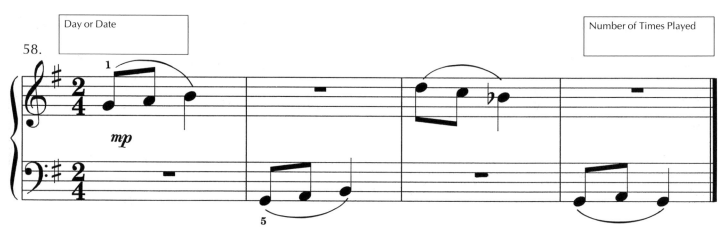

Daily Note Search

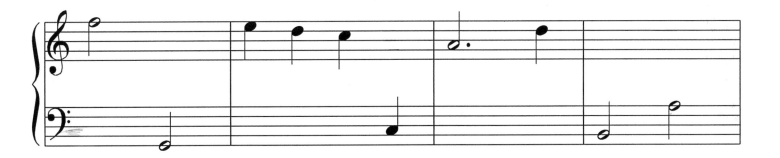

After you have sight read each line a day as usual, play lines 59, 60, and 61 without stopping. Now you are playing a long solo! What will you call it?

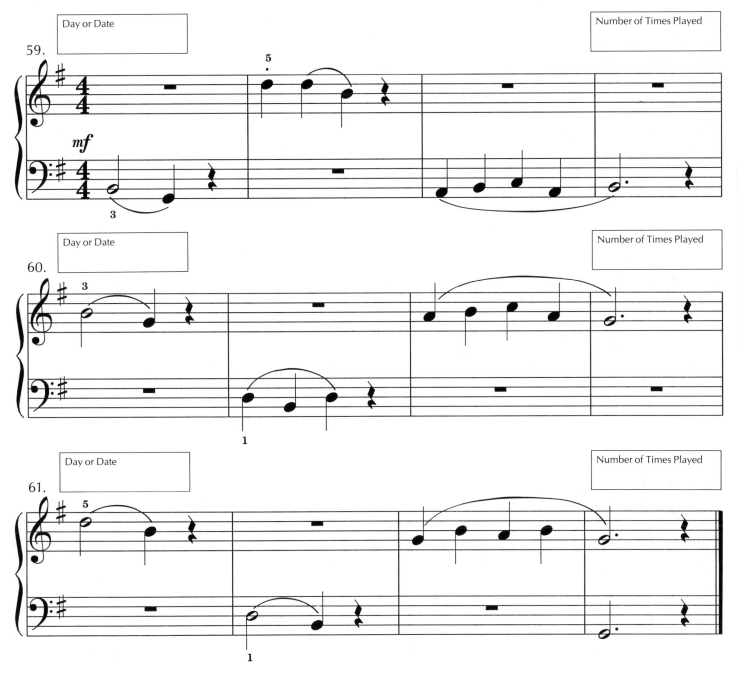

Daily Note Search

Daily Note Search

After you have sight read each line a day as usual, play lines 65, 66, and 67 without stopping. Now you are playing a long solo! What will you call it?

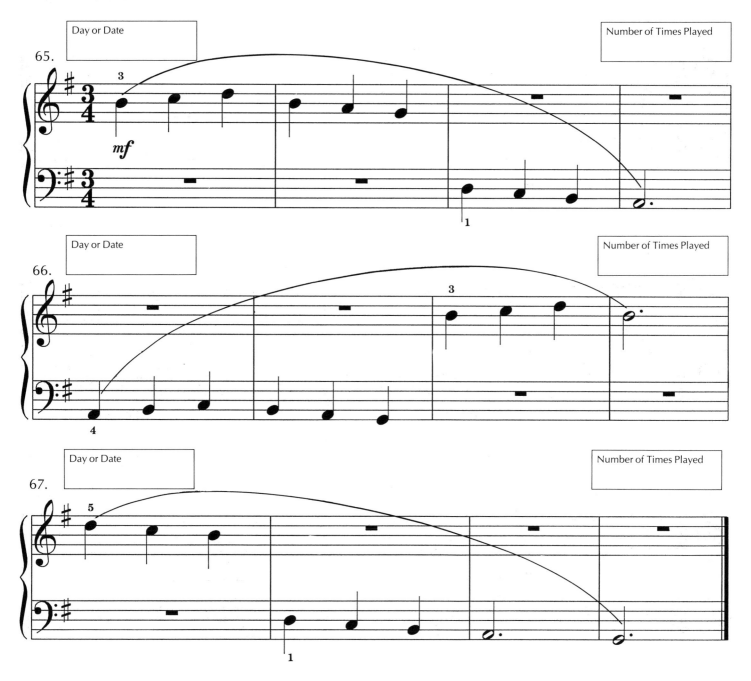

Daily Note Search

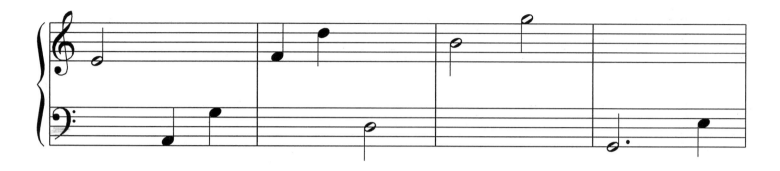

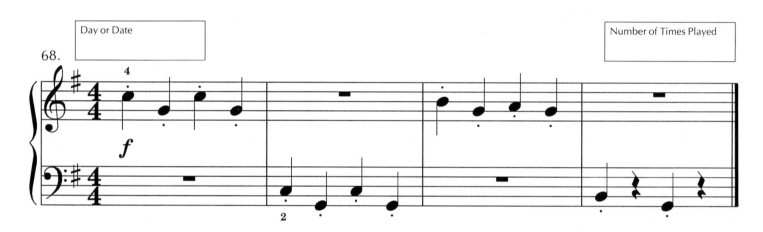

Day or Date		Number of Times Played

68.

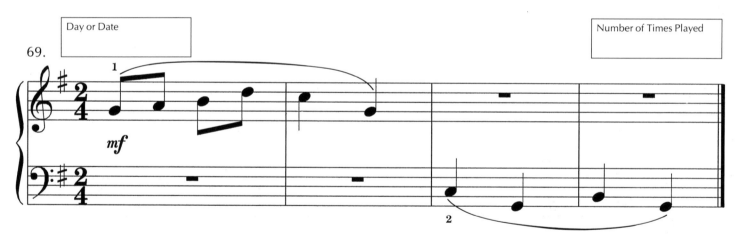

Day or Date		Number of Times Played

69.

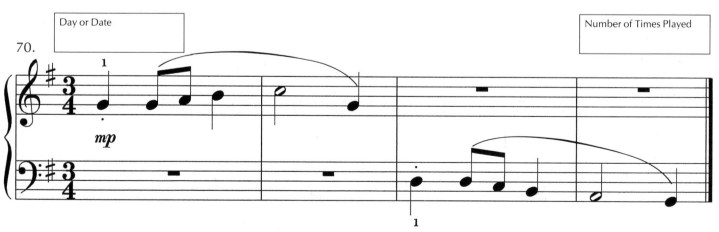

Day or Date		Number of Times Played

70.

Daily Note Search

After you have sight read each line a day as usual, play lines 71, 72, and 73 without stopping. Now you are playing a long solo. What will you call it?

Day or Date		Number of Times Played

71.

Day or Date		Number of Times Played

72.

Day or Date		Number of Times Played

73.

Daily Note Search

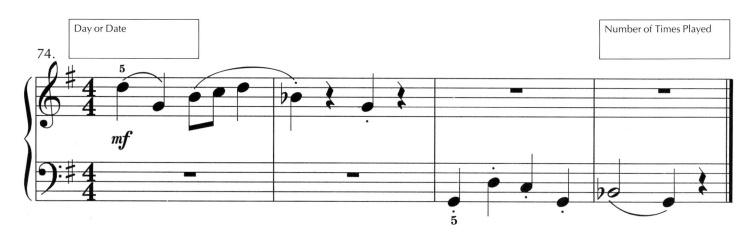

Day or Date

Number of Times Played

74.

mf

5

Day or Date

Number of Times Played

75.

mp

1

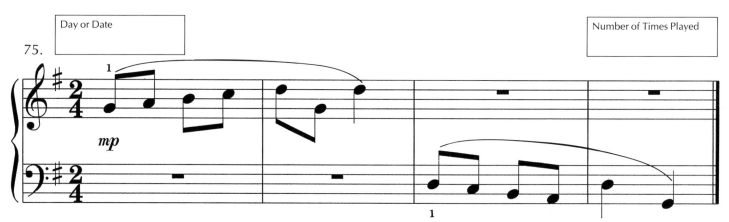

Day or Date

Number of Times Played

76.

f

4

1

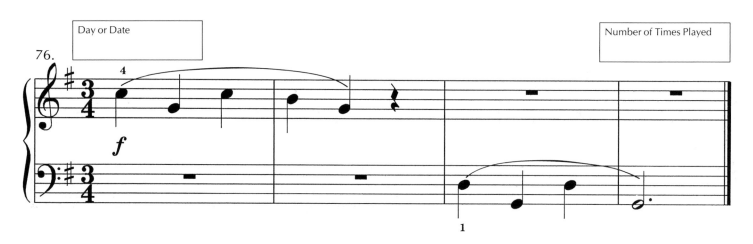

Daily Note Search

After you have sight read each line a day as usual, play lines 77, 78, and 79 without stopping. Now you are playing a long solo! What will you call it?

77.

Day or Date		Number of Times Played

78.

Day or Date		Number of Times Played

79.

Day or Date		Number of Times Played

Daily Note Search

After you have sight read each line a day as usual, play lines 80, 81, and 82 without stopping. Now you are playing a long solo! What will you call it?

Daily Note Search

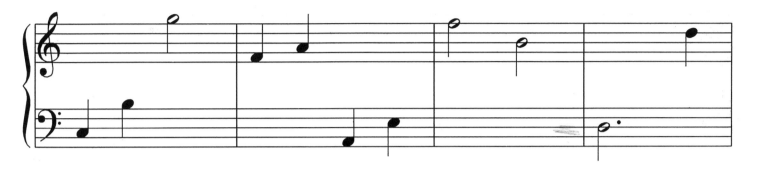

Test yourself in each position.

83.

84.

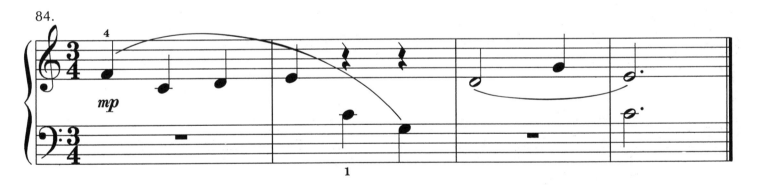

85.

Sight Reading Certificate

for

_____

who has completed Level 1 with

Honors

Superior Honors

Date_____

Teacher_____

*Honors and Superior Honors stickers are available from your favorite music store. Ask for Jane Smisor Bastien Seals, _Honor Awards_ (G2).